Full of Jewish Promise and Spiritual Adventures

FULL OF JEWISH PROMISE AND SPIRITUAL ADVENTURES

Background of Israelis, the Jewish Religion,
the Land and the Bible

Danny Teller

PARTRIDGE

To order additional copies of this book, contact
Toll Free 800 101 2657 (Singapore)
Toll Free 1 800 81 7340 (Malaysia)
orders.singapore@partridgepublishing.com

www.partridgepublishing.com/singapore

Contents

Acknowledgments

As is the custom of other writers, I thank people who have been a human treasure in my life. Under normal circumstances, such special people deserve my gratitude and acclaim for helping me make my stories epic and pulsating adventures.

But I don't feel my maternal family in the United Kingdom is worthy of anything but severe criticism and condemnation, partially due to the way they mistreated or misunderstood me from birth until I was in my midtwenties. The only exception to this has been my father, who in recent times has attempted to make peace with me.

I tried to raise a family in Israel from the early 1990s to 2002, but that was an even worse experience that nearly ended in my total collapse.

I have met a good number of intriguing strangers during my travels around the world, especially since 2002. Some of those turned out to be good friends who kept in contact with me for a while. With others, it was merely a hello or good-bye at one place or another.

I dedicate this story to Yvonne, my second wife, who is in the People's Republic of China. She had a background that left a bit to be desired, but we both take responsibility for our shortcomings. She has been truly adorable and honorable; I hope she will be my loyal friend until death do us part. She helped me settle in China; without her guidance and assistance, I could never have accomplished all that I have in China.

May God help you find peace and tranquility for ever more, amen.

—Danny Teller

Introduction

I am a British national who lives in Tianjin, China, only thirty minutes by high-speed train from Beijing. Since 2009, I have been teaching Chinese students to speak, read, and write English.

I have been a writer on and off since 1986. I have traveled internationally for well over thirty years and have written travel biographies, fiction, nonfiction, poetry, and some fairy tales.

These short stories deal with Israel from the 1980s to the early part of the twenty-first century. It's often difficult to understand the culture of Israel because the Middle East is one of the most misunderstood, volatile, and fascinating parts of the world.

Whatever is happening in Israel is due to religious and political developments that stretch back over four thousand years. Israel needs to be defined in terms of what it is fighting over and why—a piece of land. It's also an issue of who is right or wrong if indeed there is an answer to that question.

These stories help explain why the Israeli/Arab conflict is still going on at the expense of Jewish and Palestinian lives. The conflict has also indirectly affected a considerable number of people since well before the modern state of Israel was created in 1948.

Jewish people firmly claim they have solid roots and an ancestry for the right or wrong reasons. Alternatively, it could be that the phrases *Zionism*, the *Chosen People*, and the *Holy Land* are still grossly misunderstood or ill-defined.

My experiences have led me to say, "What I expected I didn't receive, and what I received I didn't expect."

Since 1985, when I immigrated there, Israel's population has increased nearly threefold. The issue of land and sovereignty is a very delicate and sensitive matter due to the country's small size.

I went to Israel on holiday a few times in the 1960s, 1970s, and early 1980s, and I fell in love with it. That was why immigration there, *aliyah*, was so attractive to me, and I lived there from 1985 to 2002.

This book is about the Middle East's splendor and glory that give rise to a variety of hopes and beliefs with fundamental issues such as being in God's country or the Holy Land.

Because of my previous holidays in Israel, I more or less knew what to expect, but my standard of life during my seventeen years there was much lower than I had expected. I was uncertain how to improve it.

Israel comprises many nationalities and religions, but Judaism, Islam, and Christianity are the main three. Of course, Jews and Arabs constitute the majority of the population; for them, fighting is a fact of life. Religious beliefs still control to a large extent how people think and behave.

In many aspects, I consider myself a Middle Eastern expert. What do I mean by that? There are considerable differences of opinions about the New and Old Testaments and the Koran, but they contain stories about the Middle East. Then there is the issue of why Israeli and Palestinian leaders still send people to fight for their country and die for the sake of patriotism. As you will learn from my short stories, I have been exposed to various sects in Israel, from the extreme right wing to the extreme left wing, from the "fascists" to the "traitors." Others define this as a battle between religious and nonreligious whether Jews or Muslims.

Judaism is defined as secular, reform, conservative, national, Hasidic (very religious) or ultra-orthodox (the most extreme). You will learn other aspects of Israeli culture as well in my stories.

Enjoy my adventures in the Middle East with all its mystical splendor, glory, and intrigue. My time in Israel included long, happy, golden days during which the Mediterranean lapped its shore. Days during which the aroma of falafel combined with the sight of Israeli soldiers searching every nook and cranny in the old but thankless Arab/Israeli conflict. Days of romance during Jewish weddings, Hasidic and traditional. War after war. Miracle after miracle. Flights over the coastline of the Holy Land that evoked rare feelings. Gorgeous women beckoning handsome men in a tiny patch of mystical, subtropical, arid, mountainous, and fertile land steeped in historical and picturesque beauty.

Israel is a land of fatal attraction. I hope my pleasure in writing is matched by your enjoyment and entertainment in reading it.

—Danny Teller
February/March 2016

1

Jewish Purity—
Taharat Hapishpaha

Jewish purity is about being clean and healthy in Jewish marriages inside and outside Israel. Purity is sacred, especially to those Jews who believe in it and preserve its righteous laws.

The time during which a wife can't have sexual relations with her husband for at least twelve days is called the honeymoon period. She can't sleep with him or touch him. Some don't allow the wife even to hand an item to her husband during this time.

Her body is considered impure when she starts her menstrual period. Normally, after five impure days, she inserts a cotton cloth into her vagina around sunset for about five minutes and checks to see if it is free of blood. If it isn't, she checks the next day.

Even if it is clean, this doesn't indicate that she can have sex with her husband. Upon the seventh clean day, the twelfth since she first began menstruating, she checks her body, especially her genitals, to make sure all is clean. If she is clean, she prepares for the *mikva*, a ritual bath of cleansing. This involves shaving some of her pubic hair, cleaning behind her ears and between her toes, and cutting long toenails and fingernails.

Some observant orthodox or *haredi* woman don't have hair on any parts of their bodies and normally wear wigs or head covers. To some, this seems extreme, but to the ultra-orthodox, it's perfectly normal.

It's said that a mikvah releases special powers of pure water, which comes directly from the rains. The water in a mikvah is just like natural springs except it's indoors and heated up.

When the woman returns from the mikvah, she can have sexual relations with her husband as much or as little as she or he wants for about eighteen days.

Orthodox Jews think there's nothing more natural than this process, which keeps Jewish marriages and the health of husband and wife intact.

2

A Seventeen-Kilometer March

In November 1986, I was a cadet in an army uniform and participating in an army induction course, *marva*, in Israel. The weather was bad—by Middle Eastern standards—after what had been a prolonged drought.

During the fifth week of our eleven-week program, we were taken to Givat Olga, a sizeable town near the coastal town of Hadera, which is about an hour by car from Tel Aviv, the financial and capital city of Israel.

We trained as combat soldiers for two days; it was tough. It was nothing but running, shouting, and pretending to shoot others. After a tiring day, we gathered around the flagpole and were told to pair up and form a line. All our equipment was with us because we were going for a stroll in the country. We carried our ammunition belts, canteens, stretchers, and automatic rifles. It was going to be a long march.

The march began about 8:00 p.m. We followed Oded, our commander, for the duration of the course. The two stretchers we were carrying were folded up for the first three or four kilometers until the order was given to open one up in just four minutes with one person lying on it. This might sound like a lot of fun, and in many ways it was, but it was nonetheless difficult.

4

We were sweating despite the cold weather, but we were still eager to go. We knew our bodies had to get used to this treatment. We carried the skin on our bodies, ammunition belts, and water bottles. No one was allowed to wear glasses or carry any valuables—watches, jewelry, or money. We carried toilet paper, but fortunately, no one needed to go.

Our pace was between a jog and a fast walk. If we slacked off, we were told to speed up. We didn't know which direction we were going. We weren't supposed to feel comfortable. This was the army.

Not everyone completed the exercise because it was extremely tough. Not all my colleagues were physically fit.

It was all about working as a team and doing what we were told. The march would end when it did, and no one bothered to ask how far we had gone until it was all over.

Oded gave the command for us to stop for thirty seconds to drink—not one second more. Most cadets asked friends to remove their water bottles from their individual pouches located in ammunition belts and give them to each other. I was sweating, but I wasn't thirsty.

The march continued. I was lucky to be carrying the closed stretcher. Our numbers had dwindled from thirty-five to about twenty-five cadets. Some had left for personal reasons, not necessarily because of their health.

Four people at a time carried the open stretcher for intervals of about thirty to sixty seconds. The cadet lying on it had the responsibility of giving the command to change. Each pair of soldiers was supposed to be of similar height, making the stretcher easier to carry at shoulder height.

We hated carrying the stretcher. Its cold metal poles dug into our shoulders as we walked at our fast pace. We put it down only once during the march. We had done it before but on marches of only four or five kilometers. Only the males were allowed to participate in this exercise because it was so demanding.

The march was an ordeal for many cadets. They had come from different lifestyles and had looked forward to this course despite knowing it was the army, not a summer camp. We couldn't recall working so physically or mentally hard during our training, but it was business as usual for our commanders. The march was to test how far we could go mentally and physically. Believe me, it was further than we had thought.

At one point, someone complained that his back was hurting. I was carrying the closed stretcher and was told to hand it to my roommate, Danny Cohen. I had to take my turn carrying the open stretcher. That was murder even if it lasted just thirty or sixty seconds considering the pace we were going. We'd have breaks only when after thirty seconds, we'd put the stretcher down and take up the poles at the other end of the stretcher for another thirty seconds of carrying it.

I was carrying the stretcher with an Australian I had met a few months before marva. The cadets had to support those they were carrying the stretcher with whether they got along or not; we had to learn to work as members of a team.

We learned to carry the stretcher with less pain, but there was always some pain involved in the task. We weren't allowed to put padding on our shoulders; the whole point of the exercise was to see what we could and couldn't do under extreme pressure even if just for a limited time.

Those in some of the parachute, infantry, or commando units build their endurance up to the point that they marched up to fifty kilometers with only seven or eight men per stretcher.

Those who were accepted into marva had had some time to mentally prepare themselves for what they knew would be a tough program. If we had a plausible reason to drop out, we could because we weren't official Israeli soldiers. But I decided to complete the course in spite of the difficulties.

I estimated we had about three minutes' rest between each carry. In a real emergency or during a full-scale war, that was nothing. Some Israeli soldiers had to carry their injured friends on stretchers for two or three days without much rest.

The longer the march continued, the more people dropped out. That put pressure on those who remained, who resented those who had given up for whatever reason. "Join the army and have some fun," we'd heard, but we weren't having any fun.

We had thirty seconds to rest and drink, but the stretcher stayed up in the air during those times.

At that point in the march, I still wasn't thirsty, but Steve Rothman, an American, had picked some pomela fruit from a tree in an orchard and sliced them up for us. How he'd found time for that I'll never know; we were under pressure.

When we reached a river, we knew that we had completed about three-quarters of our march. We'd been told we'd get wet during our march. We could have waded through the river, as it was just waist deep, but no one, not even our commanders, wanted to get wet.

Oded found a branch on the ground long enough to span the river. He was as relieved as we were. He told some cadets to put it across the river. We and all our equipment got over without anyone or anything getting wet.

I had moments on that march that made me wish I hadn't been born. We were all under pressure. Oded ordered us to not complain or talk.

About thirty minutes later, he said, "We're nearly there" (but in Hebrew of course). But it was still pitch-black. I wondered why we weren't slowing down and putting the stretcher on the ground. It turned out that there were about three or four more kilometers to the finish, not the 500 meters as we had thought. Oded had told us that just to boost our morale; we were down to ten men. The military nightmare continued. I was aching everywhere as we took turns carrying the stretcher.

At about 12:30, the march finally ended. We will never forget how relieved we were. Steve Davidovitz relieved me on stretcher carrying for the final few meters. He was one of the few Americans who participated in this program, and he was twice as strong as me. He and I were among only eight who had completed the march.

I was proud of my achievement; I had thought I was mentally and physically weaker than I should have been. I found it hard to believe I had completed it and was still standing. Steve Rothman told everyone I had complained a great deal but that I had still finished.

My experience taught me I could do whatever I thought I could. I've been tested many times since, and I've always managed to pull through.

That seventeen-kilometer walk was tough, but now, I think I might have been able to go even farther—even with the stretcher.

3

THOSE WERE THE GOOD OLD DAYS

Those were the good old days well before the modern state of Israel was formed. It was a time of great comradeship and chivalry.

Those were the good old days when young Jewish pioneers with tough spirits fought side by side—brothers in arms until death did them part.

Those were the good old days in Israel when they fought and sacrificed everything they had for their own country.

Those were the good old days when dying in battle was a sacrifice worth making.

Those were the good old days with an afterlife in heaven as had been predicted by the sages.

4

Happily Ever After

It was Tuesday, September 1, 1992, and very hot. I was in a new suit while Ruth, my bride, looked like a dazzling princess. It was a special occasion, auspicious in every sense of the word.

Our romance had started less than a year before. I was twenty-eight, and Ruth was two years younger. Getting married wasn't something I had contemplated. I was at the age when so many people were opening their eyes and seeing the world.

We weren't from the same educational background and didn't have the same outlook on life. But she repeatedly asked me to marry her and had promised to make me as happy as a prince. After some persuasion, I agreed to marry her.

The music was pulsating; we had invited family and friends to be with us on this joyous night. Tinsel, balloons, and firecrackers welcomed us as we entered the hall to cheers of "Mazel tov" and "Congratulations."

My first real wedding experience in Jerusalem was similar to this one back in September 1987. Our wedding was orthodox. The men and woman were segregated by a wall.

There were many unhappy marriages in the early 1990s, and I wondered if I was making the right decision. That might have been so. She was divorced and had two kids. I should have realized the pressure of raising two stepchildren would have been too much for me. Some might have told me I wasn't ready for this, but there was no going back.

Over 80 percent of those who had been invited were there, quite good considering the controversy surrounding our marriage in the first place. Those who came made such a noise that they sounded greater in number. People shook our hands, which made us feel great. I was about to put a ring on her finger under a black and starry night.

The ceremony, which included breaking the glass under my right foot, was over in about twenty minutes. We were officially husband and wife.

In spite of my mixed emotions, I was happy to think about the here and now, not tomorrow. I can't remember a moment that night that I wasn't smiling.

The dancing was nonstop—from when we arrived until the last person went home. It was a night to remember and savor; everyone was so happy for us.

We were supposed to live happily ever after until death parted us.

5

THE HOLY LAND

The Holy Land is a tiny strip neatly sandwiched between hostile countries; it still bursts with milk and honey, perfect complements to each other.

It was called the Land of Canaan during the time of the Jewish ancestors about four thousand years ago—Abraham, Yitzchak, and Yaakov.

The Holy Land basks in the sun for at least six months a year. There's so much more to Israel than what you can see by flying over it at 25,000 feet. There's so much more to the Holy Land than what meets the eye, so come and find out for yourself what it's all about.

Welcome to the Holy land, the land of milk and honey, the Promised Land.

6

IN THE LIGHT OF THE SPIRIT

During my many years in Jerusalem, the heavenly spirit gave me the good will to visit the Wailing or Western Wall, commonly known as the Kotel.

Many believe it is what remains of the first and second temples, and it was here, on Mount Zion, that the world was said to have begun some 6,000 years ago.

The spirit of life and light brought me to prayer in the belief that what I was doing was correct. The energy source from the wall was the holiest of holies.

The prayers of my heart and soul were answered, but not how I might have envisioned today.

I always had the spirit of light, which remained in my body for a world without end, amen.

7

A Military Inspection
in the Israeli Army

If an amusing story could be told about the Israeli army, what occurred at a military barracks on a Friday afternoon in late November 1986 would be it.

Life in the army is not always as people think it is. It was an extremely industrious and challenging time for me during that cold winter. I was participating in *marva*, a difficult military induction program that introduced immigrants to the military life and prepared them to cope with it if they enlisted.

The army had many units spread over the whole country. Our base was in the Galill, a hilly area in the northwestern part of the country. The barracks belonged to a large unit called the Gadna, which was largely responsible for training some of the current Israeli commanders and leaders.

Our leaders for the program were mostly Israelis, but not all had been born in the country. They all knew English quite well but spoke to us in Hebrew as much as possible.

Marva yud het was the name of this course, which lasted eleven weeks, but that included some leave time every two weeks.

Week five was supposed to be one of the most difficult; we would practice fighting at a place called Givat Olga,

16

which was near Hadera, a coastal town. The exercise tested our mental and physical strength to the maximum.

When it was time to go back to our base, some of us were so tired that our heads were spinning like yo-yos. We had done a great deal of shouting, which had affected my voice; I lost it once for a few days.

We had each been issued three shirts, trousers, and pairs of socks but only two pairs of boots. By the time we finished, it was already quite late on a Thursday afternoon. Most of our equipment was wet, dirty, or rusty because we had sweated a great deal even though it was winter, and we had waded waist-high in the ocean with our weapons and ammunition belts. We were left with only one clean uniform, a dry pair of boots, socks, jumper, and coat.

After lunch on Friday, we were told to prepare for inspection, which was supposed to happen before the Sabbath begun at 4:00 p.m. during that time of the year.

Sadly, due to the unruly behavior of some of the squad, my opinion of the overall morale was low. I wasn't sure why some of them had come in the first place, but regardless of what we had individually hoped to gain, as far as our instructors were concerned, we had come of our own free will.

Our commanders had done a fantastic job of teaching us some army discipline especially during inspections, weapon training, navigation, and hygiene. We were all together; we had learned to work as a team and help each other.

Though most of us had worked hard for much of the time, we weren't able to complete some tasks on time because some of the group didn't care. We were supposed to have trained just like the soldiers who were serving in potentially very dangerous places such as the security zone in the southern part of Lebanon. We might have been pretending to be soldiers, but our commanders treated us like professional fighters, and that caused stress and pressure. To add to the pressure, not everyone spoke Hebrew properly or was in the same physical and mental condition. Our commanders were well aware of this during induction day on October 27, but it was all the more incentive for us to work as a team.

We had only two hours to go before inspection, so we had a great deal of work to do. Many of us were not certain we'd manage it on time. It might have been a hard week, but the real excitement was yet to come.

Inspections are difficult in spite of what you may have seen on TV. You don't have that much time to clean everything before you'll be standing in front of your commanders. We were nervous, and we tried to stay out of someone's way; we didn't want any arguments.

Pennina was put in charge of the whole group, or in Hebrew, *machlaka*. She was known in Hebrew as the *hanich toran*, a sort of teacher or organizer.

There had been as many as eight of us to a room, which were small, but at the end, some had left. The two Mexicans and the one Canadian who had been in the room with Danny and me had left. He and I had more room, but we didn't get along that well. We were about the same age, but we had different mentalities, behaviors, and indeed attitudes toward morale.

Everyone was responsible for the cleanliness of his or her uniform and equipment, including rifle, ammunition, and sleeping bag. The army was fussy about everything we did. Our weapons were very important; our commanders paid particular attention to them. Those in a room were responsible for their room's cleanliness. We knew how to arrange our beds, fold everything properly, and face everything in the right direction. All the doors, windows, and lights had to be free of dust. Our lockers needed to be clean with nothing on them. The floor needed to be as clean and as dry as possible.

Our commanders were also vigilant about our personal hygiene. We had to be clean shaven if we didn't have a beard or moustache. The women had to have their hair in ponytails if it was long. Our commanders set the example for us.

We were taught how to wear our uniforms properly our first week. That included buttoning up our shirts, wearing blue tags on our shoulders, and tying our boots properly so the laces didn't hang out.

The army was logical in many aspects of how soldiers were treated; it was all part of the basic standards we were expected to maintain. I agreed with some of the ways the army worked; it wasn't designed for pleasure. Our commanders weren't always nice to us, but we realized they were doing their jobs twenty-four hours a day.

But the inspection was coming up in two hours, and everything was going wrong. Danny had been assigned to the kitchen and had to help the chef tidy up, and he was well behind schedule by 2:30. I had to fold his uniform and arrange his bed before I could begin on my tasks. Our uniforms were wet with sweat and salt water and dirty with mud and sand, which had to be cleaned off before I washed the floor. I was happy when Danny came back.

The only consolation for me was that I had been able to work in our room alone and had gotten it relatively clean in comparison to other rooms, especially the one next to us. Our uniforms were still damp but clean. The floor, lockers, and windows were also clean. I had even managed to shake out the blankets and beat the mattresses, so all that really remained was our rifles and ammunition belts.

Cleaning an automatic rifle properly could take up to forty minutes; that depended on its condition, and ours had been dunked in the Mediterranean and were rusty and dirty. We had to strip them down piece by piece and put them together. To make matters worse Danny Cohen barely said thank you to me for arranging his belongings and for cleaning the room.

I looked into the next room to see how two Americans, Jeff Peddie and Mark Landraw, and a South African, Cliff Rosenberg, were getting on. Their room was a mess. I couldn't imagine what they had been doing for the last hour and a half.

With only thirty minutes left, I looked at the men's toilets and saw they were in a pitiful state. The floor must have had about an inch of mud we had dragged in from our combat training. Everyone was so busy cleaning his or her room that I didn't bother asking who was responsible for the bathroom.

It suddenly occurred to me that more than half the group was still dirty because we were supposed to shower near the lavatories and get dressed in our rooms. Then we were supposed to stand for inspection in the courtyard, a few meters from the dormitories.

With no more than about ten minutes to go, Danny and I began to work on our guns, but with just five minutes to go, we had no choice but to reassemble them.

I walked back along to see the other rooms but what I saw was not a pretty sight. In one, underwear and socks were hanging on a string that spanned bunk beds. The room smelled rancid due to sweat and passed gas. And it was too cold out to open the windows.

The hallway outside of our rooms was full of rubbish. Our training in Givat Olga had taken more of a toll than we had anticipated.

We were learning the army's ways, but we weren't upholding its standards.

Five minutes to go. We were in a mad panic. Pinnina came by to tell us we had nearly run out of time. Some rooms looked respectable, but others were still in shambles.

One minute to go. Pinnina called us all outside even if we weren't dressed properly. Our commanders were approaching the courtyard.

We weren't ready for the inspection. Rubbish was all over the place, and our toilets, rooms, and bodies were in bad shape but we had to get into the courtyard. And some of us weren't wearing trousers. It was all hands on deck, but our commanders were not amused in the slightest.

Three minutes after the deadline, Pinnina was finally able to give the order to stand at attention. *Hamalcha arucha muchna lepkudatcha*, "The squad is ready for your inspection." Her voice was nervous and jittery. There was a deathly silence as Oded and Corporal Arik looked at our presentation, which was a total and utter shambles. For a few deathly moments, all we could do was keep as quiet as possible. No one knew what to do, say, or think.

I was dressed properly, but my gun was around my waist, not where it should have been at my side. My eyes were full of grit, and sweat trickled from my forehead. My mouth was dry, my throat was still croaky, my body was still hurting from the combat training, but apart from that, I was feeling fine.

I tried not open my mouth for fear that what would come out would not be an exhale but laughter. I wasn't the only one who tried to contain frustration; at least two people began to laugh.

Corporal Arik asked, *Ma matzhik?* "What's funny?"

Normally, we would have been punished by having to run around the block in thirty seconds, but at least four or five of us were only in underwear and shirts.

Oded felt that quality infantry units could pass inspection even after a hard week of physical training. I think we were one of the first *marva* programs to have been late for inspections from beginning to end. Not all of us worked as a team, and I think some in our group didn't care.

Oded decided that he had no choice but to ask us to lock up the guns in our rooms, dress properly in civilian clothes, and meet at the large hall.

The inspection might have seemed hilarious, but there could have been personnel from other bases in the country or civilians checking on the army's discipline and standards. Oden described our standards as the lowest he had ever seen. He felt there was no excuse for our having underperformed. He was the second in command of our small base, but he was responsible for our squad, and he was disappointed to say the least.

We entered Shabbat with a nice dinner party followed by some well-deserved rest. That night, I wondered why some people suffered because others didn't care. I didn't have an answer.

Twenty-four hours later, after the Sabbath was over, we had another inspection. Only that time it was at night. It was a punishment for not doing it properly earlier on.

At about 3:00 a.m., we were told to get some rest, but four people had to go on guard duty until 5:00 a.m. We were getting up then for another week of training.

I was not the only one having a restless night. There were loud noises coming from the next room; Mark Landraw, Jeff Peddie, and Cliff Rosenberg were being made to run by Corporal Arik for what remained of the night.

The next morning, Jeff Peddie told me, "Danny, I wasn't able to close my eyes the whole night. We were punished even more than the rest of the group because our room was so dirty."

Their only consolation was that Corporal Arik hadn't gotten any sleep either.

8

LIFT OFF IN THE TRUE SPIRIT

I'd booked the last seat on a flight from Ben Gurion airport near Tel Aviv to London. Just after 8.30 a.m. on July 26, 2002, the last passengers boarded and the door was closed. We taxied to the runway.

Due to unfortunate circumstances, I had totally lost control of my ten-year marriage. It was a shambles that not even a counselor could have salvaged. It was just a case of trying to survive in that madhouse in Jerusalem until I could arrange enough emergency clothes, toiletries, travel documents, and money to go to the UK.

I had to leave in secrecy while I still had some energy. Living in Israel had tested my physical and mental strength to the limit on more than one occasion. I was close to a nervous breakdown and had to leave.

Ruth and I had known our marriage would break down; it was just a question of when and how we would separate. This was partially due to the stress of trying to raise four children—far too much for both of us. We had little or nothing in common to talk about except how to raise our kids in an orthodox environment.

As far as my family knew, I was working that day in a car park not far from Jaffa Gate by the old city. Ruth knew that on a Fridays, I normally finished work at 1:00

p.m. and would be home after doing some shopping in the market.

But I was on a plane ready to depart the country. I might not have been the best father or husband, but this situation had pushed me over the limit. I thought about my kids and what would happen when they realized I had left. My daughter might just have been old enough to understand because she was six and a half, but my two-and-a-half-year-old son was still in nappies and not talking. I loved my kids; abandoning them was the last resort. I knew many other men and woman had done the same in similar circumstances.

Sitting next to me was a rather nice couple who told me they lived in Rishon leZion, a town near Tel Aviv. The name of their town means "The first to participate in real Zionism." They were going on holiday to London for seven days.

They asked what I was doing. I said, "Running away from my family and my life in Israel."

Their reaction to that sudden and astonishing news was quite sympathetic. They saw how tired I was. I had lost weight over the last few months. All they could do was wish me the best of luck in rebuilding my life.

The plane climbed into the sky. It was the first time I had flown since I had gotten married ten years earlier. Some passengers seemed excited; it could have been their first flight out of Israel.

The plane picked up speed. We passed over the Israeli coast. The summer had been a scorcher after a succession of poor winters and a prolonged and difficult drought. It was hard to believe that life in the Holy Land had been so hard for me, but ever since arriving in 1985, I had been through things very few other immigrants had. I was relieved to be leaving a dreary old life behind and to be beginning a new one. The rest of my life would be different; my heart could pump blood in my body properly and efficiently.

My Israeli friends tried as much as they could to sympathize with me because they also didn't like the stranglehold some of the orthodox factions had on their country. They told me to enjoy the flight to London.

After what had been a long and loveless marriage with Ruth in which we had frequently argued, at long last I was experiencing peace at 25,000 feet.

9

Shabbat Shalom—
Welcome to the Sabbath

Orthodox and other religious Jews in Israel and worldwide prepare and celebrate what for them is the holiest time of the week, Sabbath Kodesh, Holy Shabbat. Some consider Shabbat to be more important than even Yom Kippur, one of the holiest days in the Jewish calendar. Sabbath is twenty-five hours spent in a very special environment in which the life is portrayed in its entirety to the Torah, the Jewish people, and Israel.

I shall begin with cleanliness, a long and laborious process in most observant or orthodox families. It frequently starts on a Thursday when just a part of the shopping and cooking is done. The preparation is one of the most important times of the week.

Some Haredi, the ultrareligious, begin their preparation as early as Monday or Tuesday, while others might spend only Friday afternoon cleaning and cooking. Even those Jews who aren't so religious consider the Sabbath a special time when they can sit down, watch TV, listen to the radio, light the candles, and say the *kiddush*, a blessing. Some respect the Sabbath but don't observe it, and some treat it as any other day. Those who take it seriously celebrate it as a time of peace and tranquility. Different people celebrate it in different ways, but the Sabbath is still the Sabbath. It's always at the end of the work week, which will remain the same no matter what.

Just before the wife prepares to light the candles, a final check is carried out to make sure everything is spotless, especially in the kitchen and dining room. The next important aspect is dressing in your best and cleanest clothes. Men put on dark suits, white shirts, ties, and black bowler hats. Woman and girls wear dresses and cover their heads as a sign of ritual purity.

The table is specially prepared with a tablecloth, special bread, wine, candles, and cutlery. To prevent the tablecloth from getting spoiled, a thin plastic sheet is put over it and thrown away when the Sabbath is over on Saturday night.

The bread used for Sabbath is called *hallah*. Some bakeries make it on Thursday afternoon, but most is made on Friday so it will be fresh. Some woman make it at home. My ex-wife told me it's hard work. It's not just five minutes with flour, margarine, eggs, sugar, salt, and yeast. Once the dough is ready, you have to let it rise before you mold it into special shapes and sizes before baking.

The wine is normally bought on Thursday because it's a rather heavy item to carry and saves the hassle of bringing it home on Friday. Some families prefer grape juice while some like the real stuff. It's kept in the fridge for at least one hour before being taken out about five minutes before the men come back from the synagogue.

Enough toilet paper is cut and placed in a bag to be used as needed. It's not allowed to cut anything on the Sabbath or turn on or off lights forty minutes after the candles are lit.

A special hot plate or platter is turned on to keep the food warm; turning on the oven is forbidden. The smell of cooking fills the house with pleasant aromas, which gives the wife a good feeling after having worked hard to prepare it for nearly forty-eight hours.

There are many types of foods depending on where the Jews originated from. Some like it sweet, and others like it spicy, savory, or even sour. Some like it hot, while others like it cold. Some like simple dishes while others like gourmet fare.

While the men are in the service, the woman relax at home or go to pray. There are normally many synagogues to go to, but in the summer, the women often are outside waiting for the men to return from *davening*, praying.

Shabbat is based on the religious principle that God created the world in six days and rested on the seventh. Sunday might be the first official work day in Israel with the end of the week being either Thursday or Friday. Some people work five days a week, but others work five and a half days and thus have less time to prepare for Sabbath. Some work right up until it's time to go to the evening service.

There are two main services on Friday evening at synagogues, *mincha*, the afternoon one, and *maarriv*, which follows almost right after in the evening.

There is no special time for davening or praying; that depends on the individual. Normally on a Friday, most pray together with a break of about ten minutes for a lecture. Each one is called or known as a weekly portion or in Hebrew; it's known as Parshat Hashavoah.

The Pentateuch is the five books of Moses, which are divided into the fifty-two weeks of a lunar year. The Jewish new year is different to that of Christianity, Islam, Hinduism, Buddhism and many others. The first of the fifty-two weeks begins during the harvest or autumn festival; that is known as Simcha Torah, "Being happy with the Torah."

The weekly portions are dedicated to the first day of creation, about 5,800 years ago till the death of Moses, about 3,000 years ago. Each portion explains what happens with interpretations, questions, and answers according to each person's capability, desire, and intellect.

The Jewish calendar might date back a long time, but today, many Jews complain that one day isn't really enough to rest.

Having being married to an extremely orthodox woman, I'd seen how hard many work in the house. However, there is another way of looking at it; some women want to marry young and have as many babies as possible, which prolongs their domestic life. I think that's a heavy price to pay instead of working and developing careers. Though they may claim it's God's wish, I think it's biblical brainwashing.

They learn about Judaism through books and the media as well as at *yeshivas*, schools that teach Jewish values. They are supposed to learn about using their free will and being enterprising, but the life of the average orthodox or Haredi woman does not. They can become so engrossed in bible study that changing their mind-sets is often too hard for them.

There are only two main kinds of Jews in the world—the Ashkenazi and the Sephardic. Ashkenazi Jews originate from the so-called civilized world—Europe, America, Canada, Australia, and so on. Sephardic Jews come from the developing world of the Middle East or North Africa. The stark difference between the two has caused many needless arguments and some serious and prolonged conflicts.

But getting back to the Sabbath, services range in length from forty to sixty minutes depending on the sermons and the readings. The services are meant to draw people closer to God and purify their bodies and souls.

At dinner, the bread is usually covered with a cloth. The wine or grape juice is brought to the table, and everyone sings a special song, the Song of Angels. After this, the husband or a son who is at least thirteen recites the *kiddush*, the blessing that precedes the drinking of the wine. Everyone says amen. The husband drinks some wine and pours some for everyone else.

Once that is done, everyone goes to the kitchen to wash hands before the next blessing, which is on the bread. For some reason, it's not allowed to speak before the bread is eaten. The husband gives an additional blessing on the bread before eating some. He then hands everyone a piece.

Then, normally, the wife and the daughters bring the rest of the food. This can include salad; meats, including chicken and fish; vegetables; sauces; cakes; biscuits, and so on. Depending on the family, there can be as many as fifteen dishes served. As they eat, they sing and perhaps hear a sermon based on the Bible given by the father.

The husband's life revolves around work, study, and family. Some say this is a complete, fulfilling way to live life, but that depends on the individual.

Not all Jews know Hebrew; many live in other countries and speak other languages. Some European Jews speak Yiddish, a dialect of German. The language dates back about 2,000 years; some very orthodox Jews speak Yiddish in Jerusalem. Yiddish is also heard in New York, London, Paris and other places with large Jewish communities; it can be their first language, with the language of their countries being second and Hebrew being third.

If guests are present at the dinner table, you will hear Sholhan Sabbath, "the more the merrier." A Sabbath meal can take as long as three hours depending on whether it takes place in the winter or the summer, when it can start late.

I lived in Jerusalem on and off between 1987 and 2002. Though I might not have been that religious, I was certainly immersed in the culture and society there. Though many other religions and nations have objected to Judaism and its culture, for some Jews, nothing else matters to them.

The meal concludes with a special thanksgiving prayer to praise the God of Israel for providing food, land, and home. This prayer is the Birkat Hamazon, and it takes about three or four minutes to recite. Some say it out loud while others recite it more quietly.

There are many other rituals surrounding the Sabbath, but the whole point of Sabbath is to celebrate the seventh day, when God rested.

Many people in Israel feel there is nothing quite like the Sabbath, though not all do. Some great Jewish sages explain that only if the Holy Shabbat is kept in all its purity and saintliness will Jews be kept safe and sound. The great sages also remind us that if the whole world were to observe two consecutive Sabbaths, the holy Messiah or savior would come and the world would be at peace for eternity.

Try celebrating the Sabbath this way and decide for yourself just how holy it is.

Sabbath Shalom. Good Shabbat.

10

SUCCESSFUL DREAMS ARE MONUMENTAL AND UNABRIDGED

This story is imaginary, but similar actual events and developments in and around the World War II did happen. We begin in January 1941 during World War II and end just after May 1948, when Israel officially became a modern country.

Adolf Hitler planned to rid the world of the Jews. Many nations behaved in almost total ignorance, as if they didn't know what was happening. I'm convinced that deep in their hearts they knew the misery and suffering that was happening. But they did little to prevent the Holocaust because they didn't care because it wasn't affecting them directly. That was unfortunately just human nature.

I come (or at least came) from a traditional Jewish family on my mother's and father's side. This book is a tribute to those hardy souls who fought with all their might to save themselves from their aggressors when all hope seemed gone forever.

Though I left Israel in July 2002, I'm concerned about what happened more than sixty years ago when my father and his parents faced death for many years against Hitler's regime.

It's due to powerful Zionist beliefs that many generations are alive today. This story is dedicated to my children, Tehilla and Mordechai Teller, whom I belief are living in Israel. I want my family name to live in the minds of those I love.

Any additional characters or names mentioned in this story are fictional. I do not want to harm anyone who had my made-up names if they are living.

Let's turn our attention to Auschwitz, one of Nazi Germany's infamous extermination camps.

Hannah Cohen was a lively woman in her late teens. Her parents came from Poland and led devout Jewish lives. They were well learned in all aspects of love and marriage. She was proud of her strong family roots and the love they shared.

Avi, her husband, was an observant Jew in his early twenties. His parents were a very orthodox family with roots that stretched back hundreds of years in that part of Europe.

Despite the atrocities and deportations their village had been subject to, Hanna and Avi Cohen were married one moonlit night. He put a wedding ring on Hanna's finger and blessed her.

Such was the romance on their wedding night that both were eager to see offspring in the new dawn.

They settled down in their small house and worked their farm until one morning about six months later, Nazi storm troopers invaded their village. Given barely enough time to pack their belongings, Hanna and Avi were transported in cattle cars that transported them and many others across the Polish border into Germany.

Hanna and Avi were segregated and put to physical labor from dawn until late at night. Some prisoners had to push containers filled with the remains of bodies. The freezing winter nearly froze them beyond human endurance. Many lost limbs to frostbite.

Their diet was designed to gain the maximum use of their bodies until they died. They were rather tough; the Jews had grit and determination. They believed God and the Torah would prevail. But they weren't invincible.

Hanna and Avi prayed in their beds every night: "Hear, O Israel, the Lord is One. The Lord is one and only for ever." They would never forget the king of Israel until their dreams came true.

Many thousands perished from cold and starvation. In one detention center, only 25 percent survived because they were crammed into one small barracks in intolerable conditions. Some managed to keep alive and consequently the flame burning.

In Hanna's barracks, conditions were slightly better. The meat was not so rancid, and the guard provided warmer clothes.

It was in the minds of everyone to escape, but how? They faced killer dogs, heavy snow, ice, barbed wire fence, and beyond that a minefield.

Roll calls at 7:00 each morning revealed those who had died during the night. The final solution was taking its toll, but the Jews were undeterred. Survival was imperative at all costs; after the war, they would make their way to Palestine.

Hanna's and Avi's love for each other was as sure as the sun. They wouldn't give into remorse; they would love each other forever.

Cholera spread through the camp due to the lack of clean water; people were dropping dead. The survivors began to lose hope. Where was God of Israel when they needed him the most? Was this a punishment for not obeying the Torah? What could they do?

What had started out to be 5,000 people crammed in a small building was reduced to just 1,500 in three months. Their endurance was tested to its limits. When the spring came, there were barely enough people alive to bury the dead. Slowly but surely, they began to regain feeling in their fingers and toes. The food rations were slightly increased; that allowed them to muster up the strength to survive day to day.

Hanna and Avi had lost a lot of weight, but they were to fight yet another day. Though freedom was still a long way off, the spring gave them hope.

During the summer of 1941, some of the strongest men and woman planned an escape. Hanna and Avi planned to join a group of Zionists who wanted to break out. Hannah pretended to be a prostitute to distract a guard; Avi killed him and took his gun and the key to an arsenal. With the weapons, they killed some of the guards at the gate. They cut through the barbed wire and fled. Many mines didn't explode; the moisture had destroyed the fuses, but others killed some of the escapees. Those who escaped tasted freedom for the first time in a year.

They were determined to go to Palestine, the land of milk and honey, the land of their ancestors, Canaan.

By morning, all who had escaped were far away from Auschwitz to evade capture even by the guard dogs. To reduce the risk of capture, they separated into groups of three or four; Hannah and Avi preferred just each other's company.

The group found shelter in barns and found chickens for food and clean water. Spring turned into summer.

After about six months in the barn, Hannah discovered she was expecting a baby. She gave birth to a boy in the autumn. The family that had sheltered them called for a doctor to circumcise the boy, who was named Shimon Yaakov Cohen. His soul was purified.

The three crossed the Polish border. The farmer had paid them a bit for their hard work on the farm, but they didn't have much money. They came across a train station and snuck into a cattle car. It was a few days before they arrived in Yugoslavia. They survived on cow's milk and the cooked potatoes the farmer had given them.

As time passed, the boy grew and became strong enough to make the long boat trip to Cyprus. At the end of 1941, they joined a long list of people who were waiting at one of the ports for passage to Cyprus.

Finally, it was their turn. Avi, Hannah, and Shimon boarded a ship and traveled to Cyprus with other refugees fleeing war-torn Europe. After a month in Cyprus, they boarded a crowded ship to Yaffo, near Tel Aviv, a major port in Palestine. They arrived there in January 1942, almost a dream come true.

Unfortunately, the British, who still had a mandate over Palestine, refused to let them dock and ordered them to return to Cyprus. Conditions onboard were almost unbearable—no fresh food or water. One person jumped overboard and drowned because he was far too weak to swim. When the British saw another passenger about to commit suicide, they decided they had no choice but to allow the ship, the *Palmach*, to dock.

Once ashore, Avi and Hannah kissed the ground.

It was three years later that the war ended; after three more years, in May 1948, David Ben Gurion stood up in the first Israeli parliament and declared the modern state of Israel.

Hannah announced she was expecting their second child. They named her Sara. They were living in temporary accommodations in Tel Aviv. That was their welcome to a new land they hoped would be theirs forever. It had been foretold by Abraham, Yitzchak, and Yaakov. The dream of creating a Jewish homeland was finally within their grasp after thousands of years of persecution and diaspora.

Not long after Israel was created, Avi and many others were called up to serve in a war that was to last on and off for many years. Their dream of reaching the Holy Land had come true, but they faced battles ahead with the Arabs and the Palestinians. The war of independence in 1948 claimed the lives of more than 5,000 freedom fighters. Many more were injured.

Avi Cohen was one of the famous soldiers who returned victorious and triumphant. Not long after, Hannah gave birth to a boy, Haaim, Hebrew for "Good health!"

After his circumcision, the family and their friends enjoyed a splendid meal in celebration. Avi said the Kiddush or blessing over the wine on the Friday evening because that was the traditional way of welcoming the Sabbath. He gave the cup to Hannah to drink and then passed it to their other two children. They broke and ate hallah, the ritual bread, that Hannah had made as well.

For the time being, their lives were complete, monumental, and unabridged, amen.

11

THRILLING NIGHT

A new life was starting inside Ruth. My heart was full of peace, but I tossed and turned in our bed. Deep inside my wife, a baby boy was growing. Conception had taken place about two weeks earlier. I knew something else was alive in the room.

It was Saturday night, Sunday morning, the beginning of another week in Israel. Ruth was asleep. The three children slept in the other room.

I didn't sleep a wink. I was going to have a son.

12

White Night:
The Israeli Army, August 1988

The white, starry night of all nights was there for all to see. It was in the heat of an inky-black sky in a desert where we had what was known in our tank unit as a white night.

It was during the time when athletes were fighting for Olympic glory in Seoul that I found myself in military uniform as a member of the Israeli defense forces.

My barracks, in the desert, was considered a five-star hotel, first class by Israeli standards. Despite being off the beaten track, we were only about forty-five minutes from Eilat, the jewel on the Red Sea.

I was training to fight for my new country in the event of an emergency. I was determined to become a trained soldier, but basic tank training wasn't simple. It was not just about loading, firing, driving, commanding, and maintaining; it was also about learning how to live with other people in the union of the Holy Spirit. From about 11:00 p.m. on Thursday until 3:00 a.m. Friday, we fixed the tank inside and out.

Our tank was a Merkavah 2, which means "To build." During that period in Israel's military history, it was one of the most sophisticated tanks in the world.

Tanks have been described as safe places to fight, but they're also known as soldiers' graveyards. It was equipped with a huge cannon, large bombs, three machine guns, and a bazooka that fired small bombs into the night to make it look as if it were day.

We carried lots of ammunition as well as spare parts, camouflage, water, food rations, navigation equipment, and radios. Ours was a complete fighting unit that could be our home for up to three weeks at a time.

During the white night, we cleaned, repaired, ran, washed, tightened, listened, and learned. We did whatever our commander told us to do without question.

Seven soldiers were normally assigned for daily and weekly maintenance, but during the next training session, that number would be whittled down to four.

We were having a white night once every fortnight for what we believed to be a good cause. There were many new faces to get acquainted with, and that was done under extreme pressure and time limits.

We were there all night with our commanders to maintain our tanks to high standards for possible battle. We all knew that in the unfortunate event of a major war, we would be called up to fight for our country. We might win or lose, but we needed training and guidance.

On that white night, I called myself a true Zionist, a lover of the Jewish homeland to which I belonged.

The soldiers I was serving with were just eighteen or nineteen. They belonged to a religious unit and believed in their religion, country, and people. They were well behaved; they rarely argued about guard or kitchen duty even when they were exhausted.

We took the smaller guns off to clean them and put them back when they were ready to use again.

There was always something to do, so if we were late, we ran as punishment. We often got very messy with dirt, oil, and sweat.

A white night was nevertheless physically and mentally exhausting. Every now and again, we had inspection to inform our commanders of our progress.

We drank a lot of water because it was hot. If someone laughed while we were drinking water, he had to drink another bottle. That might sound funny, but it wasn't.

Most of our immediate commanders were sergeants fully trained to deal with new tank recruits. They used methods of discipline some of which we didn't like.

It was intriguing to learn all about tanks, but it wasn't a pleasure.

On that white night, we had a good look at the communications. Each tank was equipped with at least one radio that had to be in good working order at all times.

I often wondered what I was doing in a desert in the dead of a white night. But take the challenge; join the Israeli army and find out what a white night is all about.

On white nights like this, our immediate commanders had their superiors putting pressure on them; we were all under pressure.

We learned that a tank is perfectly safe as long as you know how to maintain it and fight with it. On this white night of all nights, we learned another important fact. Tanks were made to last and for people to live inside them and help fellow soldiers outside them.

The life of a tanker wasn't so easy, but it toughened me up, especially after a sleepless night.

A white night is no joke. But night became day, and we returned to our barracks and prepared for morning inspection.

Our faces were full of yawns and bleary eyes. Our white night was nearly over. We took off our dirty clothes and stepped into the showers.

Once our bodies were clean, we made sure our rooms were clean too.

No one looked forward to white nights. As we shook the cobwebs from the blankets and put on our clean uniforms, we considered it history.

13

ISRAEL AND ZIONISM

I have Jewish roots though I had been living outside Israel for six years. I hope not to sound pompous or impolite, but these are my opinions about modern Israel.

When I was twenty-one, I moved to Israel full of ideas about preserving the cultural, Zionist, and civil rights of the Jewish people. I was looking forward to the challenge and went about living there in a cultured and dignified way. A lot of media coverage has put Israel in the spotlight for more than one reason.

With dreams, salutations and a faith that could move mountains, I left the UK in 1985. Many people asked me if I had taken leave of my senses. They might have been right about that, but I didn't pay attention to them. Many other intrepid travelers had gone there hoping to live challenging lives.

I was eager to learn about the Jewish people, their land, and their religion. I wanted to be a Zionist, though I wasn't sure what that meant.

Some consider Zionism an idealistic dream, and the Torah a fairy tale about the rules you are supposed to obey or be condemned by the almighty God. Zionism and the Torah can be good, but I think commentaries on the Torah have grossly misrepresented it for centuries.

Though my educational background was not the best, I lived in Israel for seventeen years. The reason I stayed for so long had not been mine, but while I was there, I changed my values as a Jew and a human being.

The Middle East is steeped in mystery, suspense, and wonder, but the external and internal conflicts that go on there are unnecessary. What are the Jews and Palestinians fighting over? A small piece of land both are convinced is theirs. What right did any nation have to Israel based on a book that had been written thousands of years ago?

It has been said that Jews consider themselves a chosen people, but I have trouble defining "chosen people." Some Jews claim to be superior to other nations or people. I wasn't happy with this narrow mindedness that I consider racist. What right do I or anyone else have to look down on those who aren't Jewish or Catholic, Muslim, or Hindu for that matter?

During the early years of its modern existence, Israel was a good place to live, but only about twenty years later, Jewish values, the interpretations of its religion, and the Zionist mentality caused it to go downhill. But due to my firm belief that Israel was my home, I stayed on some *kibbutzim*, farming communities, for a while. I studied Hebrew for half a day and worked the other half. I also completed one army induction course of eleven weeks' duration and almost two years in the military.

People who go to Israel seem to be under the illusion that it's the land of milk and honey, the Holy Land. Due to Israel's geographical location, many consider it to be where time began. I don't mind if people believe this as long as they don't go to war over it.

During my time in Israel, I visited Egypt, which was actually more interesting in some respects than was Israel. In Israel, I learned a great deal about myself despite my dislike of how uneducated Israelis acted.

I supposed Israel's modernization had ended some of the corruption, but many communities still blamed each other for the current state of internal and external affairs.

My dream about the Zionist state of Israel didn't materialize, but I wish those who still hold those dreams good luck.

Many *olim*, Hebrew for "immigrants," still move there, but unfortunately, a great many also leave. Israel is not the easiest place to live even for the mentally and physically tough because of the ongoing conflicts.

The battles they have fought have resulted in many deaths on both sides. Israel has inflicted heavy casualties on the Palestinians due to their superior weaponry.

If the Palestinians really want autonomy in Israel, I wonder what they would be willing to do for that. Secular and religious Israelis fight each other, and I'm sure there are such divisions among the Palestinians. The reality is that the two peoples need each other. The media might project Arabs and Jews as hating each other, but I think Palestinians are sometimes treated much better by Israelis than by their own people, and yet they still want to destroy Israel and push the Jews into the Mediterranean forever.

After seventeen years in the Middle East and ten years of marriage to an Israeli woman, I consider myself an expert in foreign affairs; I was thoroughly absorbed in different societies during that time.

The Middle Eastern conflict might never come to a peaceful conclusion, but Israel is still Israel. I hope for my children's sake that peace will ultimately reign in the area and all neighbors will respect each other. I hope the Holy Land might become a true Zionist dream and last forever, amen.

14

SIGNING ON WITH THE ISRAELI ARMY

The skies were inky black. The bus I was traveling in with other new recruits arrived at Tel Hashomer or Bakum, Israel's main induction center in Tel Aviv.

When we arrived, we were told to walk to the first of many buildings and tents. The process of recruiting soldiers normally took between forty-eight and seventy-two hours depending on many factors, including where they wished to go for basic training.

We civilians were about to sign official military documents and change into uniforms. I was nervous, but I wasn't alone in that. I was about 60 or 70 percent fluent in Hebrew, which meant I understood enough to know what was happening. That was pretty good considering I had been in Israel for less than two years, only a proportion of which was spent in a totally Hebrew-speaking environment such as this.

Many think Israel is hot and dry all year around. It can be in the twenties and thirties centigrade during the summers, but the winters can be rainy.

I had arrived in the country only a few days prior to signing on, so I didn't have much time to mentally and physically prepare myself for the big adventure. I was twenty-three, older than other recruits, who were generally in their late teens.

I got a haircut and received my personal identification number I was to use during my service and reserve duty in years to come.

I had enlisting for just twenty-one months instead of the usual three years; my release date was in November 1989. What would happen between that day and November 1989 was up to me. But my commanders had to make decisions about my health, level of proficiency in Hebrew, marital status, profession, and which unit to send me to.

This was the army. I felt good about doing something I considered the correct thing to do. I knew that my bed wouldn't be a comfortable one in a heated bedroom. I knew I wouldn't have a thick blanket; that was considered a luxury in the army.

We slept in tents that held nine soldiers. The blankets were dirty. The sleeping bags weren't particularly comfortable. The springs on the cold metal beds were loose. Such conditions caused some soldiers to wake up with bad coughs, colds, and sore backs.

My pre-military training in 1986 and 1987 had given me a taste of the military life and the duties that were expected of me, but it wasn't surprising that many soldiers refused to serve in some risky parts of the country.

My mother had been afraid of my getting killed or injured, but I reminded her that any normal army sends soldiers to fight only if they are fully trained and qualified for combat.

One of the many army rules stipulates that males who are only sons aren't allowed to be fighters or to go into any combat unit even they wanted to. This is due to the compensation the army would have to pay to the families in the case of a death.

Being in the army carried more risk than civilian life did, but I had made the decision to do it then rather than later.

I saw a dentist and was photographed, fingerprinted, and vaccinated against jaundice and tetanus. I also had to let my immediate commanders know where I was every moment.

I signed for a uniform and found myself among soldiers who were asked to check the contents of what we had received, which included our kitbags. I was officially an Israeli soldier but with a foreign background, mentality, and language. There were other immigrants in the army even though they weren't obligated to sign up.

In my group was an eighteen-year-old who was of South African origin; he was in for the full three years. He told me of his desire to go into the intelligence unit. I told him a possibility for me was the tank corps.

The number of immigrants in the Israeli army was moderately low in the mid- to late 1980s compared to what it became ten to twenty years later.

I had come to Israel in 1985 and had absorbed cultural and ethnical shocks during my time as a civilian. Some of the lovely or unexpected surprises had freaked me out, but I enjoyed a number of them. It was hard for me to say how happy I was then or should have been, but that was really up to me and my attitude.

I had a thirst for adventure in Israel and was certain there were plenty more adventures to come. For instance, our first instruction was about *handasa cravi*, minefields, and their purpose in war. My fun in the military was just beginning.

The rains kept up. My introduction to the Israeli military was chilly.

Most of what we receive we don't expect, and most of what we expect we don't receive. My time in the military was no exception to that rule.

15

GOD'S COUNTRY

Israel, here I come, I thought. My future was all mine for the taking. What a fantastic feeling it was to fly over the coast. I had traveled many lands before I arrived back in my homeland.

This is God's country as prophesized in the Bible, a land bursting with so much dynasty and travesty. I was finally back. I had been reborn and had come back to Israel, my country for ever and ever, amen.

Epilogue

I hope you have thoroughly enjoyed this book. Please come back onboard for the next one and the one after that so help me almighty and living God.

I wrote this book for my intrepid and loyal readers. I'm delighted you took the time to read it.

You might be wondering when my next book will be out. I write on many topics; I'm never sure what I will write about next. But I always want my writing to capture and entertain the general public.

These mystic, epic stories about Israel contain only part of the mystery of the Middle East. I plan on writing an autobiography about my time in Israel.

My mind is bursting with many more pros and cons about the Jewish homeland, my favorite country and what I hope will become my permanent home.

I hope you will visit Israel; the Promised Land is yours for the questioning, asking, and taking.

On behalf of peace and enlightenment, I, Danny Teller, thank you. I hope you will read my next stories. Until then, good-bye and good luck.

Printed in the United States
By Bookmasters